Totally Topical

Hooray for Harvest!

Sheila Wilson

Topical ideas by Maureen Hanke

Novello Publishing Limited
8–9 Frith Street, London W1V 5TZ

I dedicate this song collection to members of my family:
Mary and Peter; Sylvia and Arthur; and Jean
with very much love to you all.

A matching tape cassette of the music is also available
(side A with vocals, side B with vocals omitted)
from Redhead Music, Juniper House, 25 Spinfield Park,
Marlow, Bucks SL7 2DD (tel. 01628 473806).

Visit the Music Sales Internet Music Shop at
http://www.musicsales.co.uk

Exclusive distributors:
Music Sales Limited, Newmarket Road
Bury St Edmunds, Suffolk IP33 3YB
All rights reserved.

Order No. NOV200205 ISBN 0-85360-711-7
© Copyright 1996 Novello & Company Limited.

Music set by Seton Music Graphics.
Cover illustration by Rodney Forss.
Cover design by Jon Forss.
Printed in the United Kingdom by
Caligraving Limited, Thetford, Norfolk.

HOORAY FOR HARVEST!

Words & music
by Sheila Wilson

With movement ♩ = 132

mf brightly

1. Hoo - ray___ for har - vest!

Jump for joy!___ Hoo - ray___ for har - vest, Each girl and boy!

Hoo - ray___ for har - vest! Twist and shout! Come and let us tell you What it's

* Optional instrumental verse can be added before verse 4 if required.

4. Hoo - ray___ for har - vest! Jump for joy!___

Hoo - ray___ for har - vest, Each girl and boy! Hoo - ray___ for har - vest!

Touch your toes! It's all a - bout the farm - er And the food he

grows!

5

HOORAY FOR HARVEST!

1.	Hooray for harvest!	*Optional actions*
		spread hands out*
	Jump for joy!	*jump*
	Hooray for harvest,	
	Each girl and boy!	*point twice*
	Hooray for harvest!	
	Twist and shout!	*do the twist*
	Come and let us tell you	*beckon*
	What it's all about!	
2.	Hooray for harvest!	*(as above)*
	Jump for joy!	
	Hooray for harvest,	
	Each girl and boy!	
	Hooray for harvest!	
	Lend a hand!	*thumb to shoulder*
	We're digging and we're weeding	*dig*
	To prepare the land!	
3.	Hooray for harvest!	*(as above)*
	Jump for joy!	
	Hooray for harvest,	
	Each girl and boy!	
	Hooray for harvest!	
	Turn around!	*jump round*
	We take a seed and plant it	*plant a seed*
	Deep within the ground!	
4.	Hooray for harvest!	*(as above)*
	Jump for joy!	
	Hooray for harvest,	
	Each girl and boy!	
	Hooray for harvest!	
	Touch your toes!	*touch toes*
	It's all about the farmer	*crouch then 'grow'*
	And the food he grows!	

*repeat each time this line occurs

6

Topical ideas

- Festivals of the Christian Church are often closely linked with natural events in our society. **Harvest** is a good example. Traditionally, harvesting is completed sometime between the first ripe corn of August and 29th September, the feast of St Michael. Discuss which the main cereal plants are that we grow and harvest.

- At **Michaelmas** it is traditional to eat roast goose stuffed with apples. Freshly baked bread is eaten with the meal, and plenty of wine and beer is drunk. Apple pie and cream follow for pudding. A bumper feast to celebrate two important events: the end of the harvest and the feast of St Michael.

A Celebration In Music

Using the notes C to C, establish an 8 note ostinato played as two bars of common time (rather like church bells). For example:

Next, add shorter scale passages of different lengths, repeating over the ostinato, keeping the steady beat. Use up to six different players, depending on how big your celebration is! Here are some ideas to get started:

When the piece is established, add the lowest sounding C that you have (perhaps an octave C at the bottom of the piano) on the first beat of each bar. After four bars, change it to an F and after four more bars to a G. Continue to rotate round these three notes and listen to the harmonic effect.

- **Bells** often feature in musical celebrations. Listen to the end of Tchaikovsky's *1812 Overture*. A different style of bells is heard in Avo Part's *Cantus in Memory of Benjamin Britten* (EMI). The piece is a descending A minor scale played at different speeds.

HARVEST MOON

Thoughtfully ♩ = c.150

1. Har - vest moon,___ shine down on me,___ (2.) That
2. Har - vest moon:___ to us a sign,___
4. Har - vest moon,___ since time be - gan,___

Shed your light___ for all to see.___
gold - en fields___ have reached their prime.___
You have seen___ the ways of man.___

*Verse 3 = piano instrumental.

8

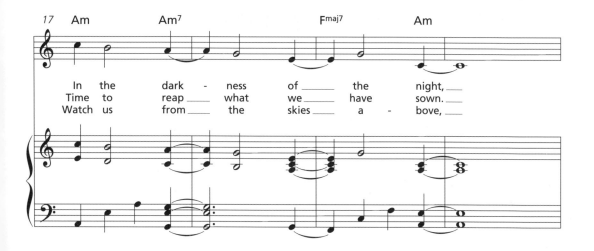

17 Am · Am⁷ · F^maj7 · Am

In the dark - ness of ____ the night, ____
Time to reap ____ what we ____ have sown. ____
Watch us from ____ the skies ____ a - bove, ____

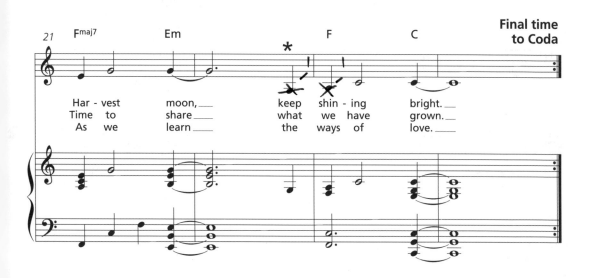

21 F^maj7 · Em · * · F · C · **Final time to Coda**

Har - vest moon, ____ keep shin - ing bright. ____
Time to share ____ what we have grown. ____
As we learn ____ the ways of love. ____

Coda

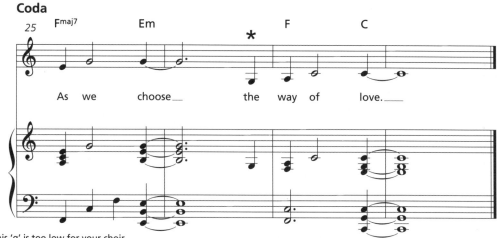

25 F^maj7 · Em · * · F · C

As we choose ____ the way of love. ____

* If this 'g' is too low for your choir,
substitute an 'e' instead.

9

repeat

HARVEST MOON

1. Harvest moon, shine down on me,
    Shed your light for all to see.
    In the darkness of the night,
    Harvest moon, keep shining bright.

2. Harvest moon: to us a sign,
    That golden fields have reached their prime.
    Time to reap what we have sown.
    Time to share what we have grown.

3. Harvest moon, since time began,
    You have seen the ways of man.
    Watch us from the skies above,
    As we learn the ways of love.

    As we choose the way of love.

Topical ideas

- A **harvest moon** is a particularly bright moon during harvest time. If rain was expected it was often necessary to work through the night, so the light of the moon was very useful to the harvesters.

- Before Christianity, it was believed that if the **reaper** who worked on the last sheaf in the field was slain and his blood used to enrich the soil, it would ensure a good harvest next year. Today, the image of a skeleton with a scythe still symbolises death. At the end of the year the same image becomes Old Father Time, who sees the old year out.

- **Night** has been depicted in music in many different ways. In the *Dance Macabre* by Saint Saëns, night is associated with the devil playing his violin. In *The River Moldeau* from Smetana's *Ma Vlast*, the river is depicted in moonlight using high pitched melodies on muted violins. *Moonlight*, the third *Sea Interlude* by Benjamin Britten, is atmospheric in a different way. **Listen** to extracts of all of these and decide which you like best.

Night Music

Make up your own piece of **programme music** (music that tells a story, paints a picture or creates a mood). You can use the words of this song as a starting point, or perhaps a picture of the night. Consider how you'll capture in sound the detail of the subject, and your feelings about the night:

- will the music have melodies?
- will it have chords?
- will it be fast or slow?
- will it use a regular beat?
- what about dymanics?
- are there any interesting sounds you can use on the electric keyboard?

How will you record the piece? Perhaps with a tape recorder, or notate it using your own symbols.

FOOD CHAIN BLUES

food   chain   blues   I'm   talk - in' a - bout!____

Optional piano solo. Go to bar 53 to omit.

* Blues are traditionally sung low, so try to sing the lower line if possible.

2. Well if you think it's dull,

You'd be ___ right, ___ Sit - ting in the

dirt ___ Day and ___ night. ___

Food chain ___ blues, ___ Food chain ___ blues, ___

FOOD CHAIN BLUES

1. The farmer sows the seed
   In the ground.
   The farmer sows the seed
   In the ground.
   Food chain blues,
   Food chain blues,
   That's what keeps the world
   A-turning round.
   You grow the food and eat it.
   No one can beat it!
   It's the food chain blues I'm talkin' about!

   Oooh yeah!

2. Well if you think it's dull,
   You'd be right,
   Sitting in the dirt
   Day and night.
   Food chain blues,
   Food chain blues,
   And when I fin'lly make it
   To the light.
   They cut me down and eat me,
   The system really beats me!
   It's the food chain blues I'm talkin' about!

   Yeah. . .

Topical ideas

- The **food chain** is a term describing the natural process whereby smaller organisms (living things) become food for larger organisms, as a source of energy. For example, grass is eaten by rabbits, who are eaten by foxes. This song takes a light-hearted view of life as a grain of wheat, at the bottom of the chain.

- **Corn dollies** are one of the best known customs associated with harvest. It was believed that the Corn Spirit (who was also the spirit of fertility) hid in the growing corn. As the field was cut, the harvesters would leave the final row of corn standing for the Corn Spirit to hide in. The row would be cut by the Lord of the harvesters or an old respected worker, who would fashion it into a dolly in which the Corn Spirit was protected. The following spring it was crushed and sown with the new seed, and so the Corn Spirit returned to the land.

- **Listen** to any of the great jazz players to hear improvisations: Louis Armstrong, Dizzy Gillespie, Sonny Rollins, Miles Davis or Charlie Mingus.

A Blues Improvisation

Start by playing a walking bass line, quite slowly:

Take it in turns to improvise over the top with any notes from the following scale, using lots of different rhythm patterns.

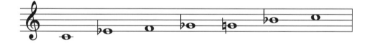

For contrast, change the walking bass line to start on an F and try improvising with notes from the same scale starting on F:

BRING YOUR CHILDREN HOPE

Close your eyes, And pray with me, For all the child-ren We can-not see, Who have no food, To

BRING YOUR CHILDREN HOPE

Close your eyes,
And pray with me,
For all the children
We cannot see,

Who have no food,
To call their own;
Many even
Have no home.

Father God,
We ask you please,
To send them food
To meet their needs,

Show us how we,
So far away,
Can help to change
The world today.

You have given
So much to us;
Please dear God
In whom we trust,

Send them seed,
And sun and rain,
So that they can
Grow the grain,

Chorus (divisi)
And bring your children hope again.
   Bring Your children hope again.
Bring Your children hope,
Bring Your children hope again.
Bring Your children hope.

You have given
So much to us;
Please dear God
In whom we trust,

Show us how we,
So far away,
Can help to change
The world today.

Chorus (divisi)
And bring Your children hope again.
   Bring Your children hope again.
Bring them hope
   Bring Your children hope,
Bring them hope   *repeat*
   Bring Your children hope again.
Bring them hope
   Bring Your children hope,

Bring Your children hope again.

Topical ideas

- **Children** in the country often used to miss school because they were needed to work on the farm. Harvesting local fruit or grain was so important that school holidays were built around them. Pea picking in some areas started in June/July, followed by fruit picking. But the most significant time for all was the harvest. One school log book from Launton, Oxfordshire, sums it up in 1862. The head teacher recorded that the school summer holiday would be set for 16th August: 'this is later than usual as the corn is backward this year owing to the wetness of the season'.

- **Read** Louisa M. Alcott's description of apple picking in *Good Wives*: 'There were a great many holidays at Plumfield and one of the most delightful was the yearly apple picking'...

- Harvesting food isn't a happy time if the crops have failed or if you don't get any food. **Listen** to a recording of *God Bless the Child*, by Janis Ian, in which she expresses the inequalities in the world, including its food distribution.

- Every day thousands of people around the world go hungry. Every day people die of diseases that a good diet could prevent. The biggest **famine** this century was in Africa in 1985 when hunger threatened the lives of 10 million people. A famine is when an area of people who can usually feed themselves suddenly cannot. Nature triggers a famine (if there is less rainfall than normal, for example) but people need to work together to prevent it. Countries that are prone to extreme weather conditions need protection against drought or floods.

- Find out how our government helps with world aid. The Secretary of State for Foreign Affairs is responsible for overseas aid and development projects. A good starting point would be to write to him/her at the Foreign Office in Whitehall. What other organisations and charities do you know that help people in vulnerable parts of the world? Can you think of ways in which you can help people overseas who suffer from lack of food?

Music for the Children of the World

Here are some rhythm patterns from different parts of the world. Try playing each of them as an ostinato pattern on its own, then see if any will fit together:

1. This is called Gota; it's from Ghana, West Africa:

2. An Irish jig:

3. A Scottish snap rhythm:

4. A South American calypso rhythm:

Make a list of songs and pieces of music that you know and see if you can identify where in the world each comes from.

HOORAY FOR HARVEST!
Finale

HOORAY FOR HARVEST!

Finale

1. Hooray for harvest!
    Jump for joy!
    Hooray for harvest,
    Each girl and boy!
    Hooray for harvest!
    Touch your toes!
    It's all about the farmer
    And the food he grows!

2. Hooray for harvest!
    Jump for joy!
    Hooray for harvest,
    Each girl and boy!
    Hooray for harvest!
    Stamp your feet!
    Praise the Lord for giving us
    The food we eat!

3. Hooray for harvest!
    Jump for joy!
    Hooray for harvest,
    Each girl and boy!
    Hooray for harvest!
    Please don't cry:
    We've reached the end, so join us
    In a big good-bye!

Optional actions
spread hands out*
jump

point twice

touch toes

} *crouch then 'grow'*

(as above)

stamp feet

} *rub tummy*

(as above)

touch corner of eye

} *wave*

*repeat each time this line occurs

6/98 (31049)